MUSIC FROM AND INSPIRED BY

Disney · PIXAR

SOUL

JAZZ COMPOSITIONS AND ARRANGEMENTS BY JON BATISTE

ISBN 978-1-70512-820-6

Visit Hal Leonard Online at
www.halleonard.com

Contact us:
Hal Leonard
7777 West Bluemound Road
Milwaukee, WI 53213
Email: info@halleonard.com

In Europe, contact:
Hal Leonard Europe Limited
42 Wigmore Street
Marylebone, London, W1U 2RN
Email: info@halleonardeurope.com

In Australia, contact:
Hal Leonard Australia Pty. Ltd.
4 Lentara Court
Cheltenham, Victoria, 3192 Australia
Email: info@halleonard.com.au

MUSIC FROM AND INSPIRED BY

Disney · PIXAR
Soul

Performed by Jon Batiste:

Jazz Standards:

Bonus Selections:

BORN TO PLAY

By JON BATISTE

Uptempo Swing

* Recorded a half step higher.

COLLARD GREENS AND CORNBREAD STRUT

By JON BATISTE

Recorded a half step lower.

LOOKING AT LIFE

By JON BATISTE

FRUIT OF THE VINE

By JON BATISTE

IT'S ALL RIGHT

Words and Music by
CURTIS MAYFIELD

SPIRITUAL CONNECTION

By JON BATISTE

Medium Swing, half-time feel

With pedal

* Recorded a half step lower.

Instrumental solo

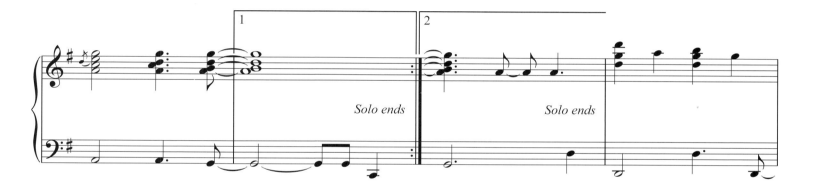

Solo ends   *Solo ends*

CRISTO REDENTOR

By DUKE PEARSON

Slow half-time feel

EPISTROPHY

By THELONIOUS MONK
and KENNY CLARKE

I LET A SONG GO OUT OF MY HEART

Words and Music by DUKE ELLINGTON,
HENRY NEMO, JOHN REDMOND
and IRVING MILLS

Slowly, with an easy Swing

Ev - 'ry - one has a fa - vor - ite song,

my heart has one, too; ___

but I lost my

BLUE RONDO A LA TURK

By DAVE BRUBECK

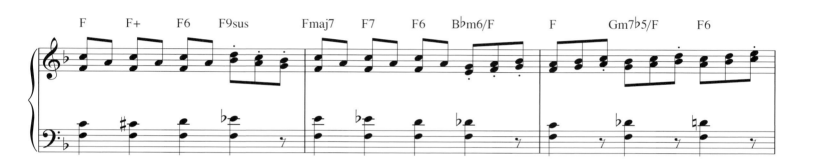

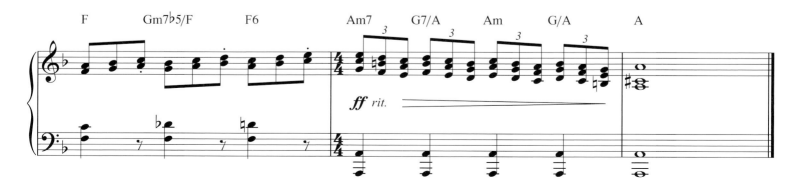

DANCELAND

By EARL "BUD" POWELL

poco rit.

EPIPHANY

Music by TRENT REZNOR
and ATTICUS ROSS

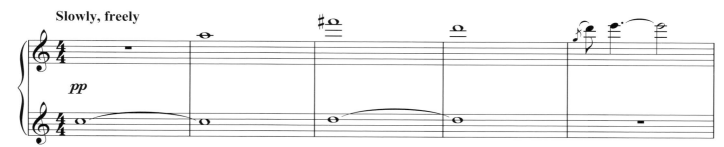

PARTING WAYS

Words and Music by
CODY CHESNUTT

*Recorded a half step higher.